Palestine in My Heart

Poems and Sculptures

Pitika Ntuli

First published by Botsotso in 2025
59 Natal St
Bellevue East
Johannesburg 2198
botsotsopublishing@gmail.com
www.botsotso.org.za

ISBN: 978-0-6398785-0-8

in the text©PitikaNtuli
the photographs©PitikaNtuli

Acknowledgements:
Thank you to Dr. Cassius Lubisi, Prof DBZ Ntuli, Simphiwe Ntuli and Saber Ahmed Jazbhay for accompanying me on my journey.

Editing: Allan Kolski Horwitz
Layout and Design: Vivienne Preston - Advance Graphics
Photographs: John Hodgkiss

Cover: Memories of Home and Exile - Quartz
Typeface: Poems; 10pt Myriad Pro Regular
         Headings; 12pt Myriad Pro Bold

THINA SOBABILI — Together!
Introduction to "Palestine in My Heart"

They are huddled not just for warmth,
but for remembrance.
For a heartbeat that defies the drone,
for a whisper that resists the thunder
of missiles dressed as policy.

They hold each other like broken stars
trying to reform a constellation—
not just of survival,
but of spirit.

These children,
these mothers,
these lovers under siege,
are not statistics.
They are Thina Sobabili
entangled in one breath,
bone of bone,
prayer of prayer.

They do not cry alone.
Their tears trace ancient rivers
from Gaza to Sharpeville,
from Jenin to Boipatong.

Their hope, however faint,
is not foolish.
It is the last wild seed
buried in scorched soil
still daring to bloom.

We are them. They are us.

Thina Sobabili — together
when they huddle for safety,
we must huddle for truth.
When they reach for peace,
we must raise sculpture and stanza.
When they whisper God's name
through smoke and blood,
we must answer
with our own names
made holy by solidarity.

Pitika Ntuli

Babuthene hhayi nje ngenxa yokufudumala,
kodwa ngenxa yokukhumbula.
Ngokushaya kwenhliziyo okumelana nezinhloli,
ngokuncwasa okuphikisa iziqhumane
ezihambisana nenqubomgomo yobugovu.

Babambelela njengeningizimu yezinkanyezi eziphukile
bezama ukuphinda bakhe inkanyezi entsha
hhayi nje ukusinda,
kodwa umoya.

Lezi zingane,
labomama,
laba abathandekayo abaphila ngaphansi kwempi
abasiwo amanani.
Bangu Thina Sobabili
siboshelwe emoyeni owodwa,
ithambo nethambo,
umkhuleko nomkhuleko.

Abakhali bodwa.
Izinyembezi zabo zigeleza njengemifula yakudala
kusukela eGaza kuya eSharpeville,
kusukela eJenin kuya eBoipatong.

Ithemba labo, noma lingathenjwa,
alilona iphutha.
Yimbewu yokugcina yasendle
ethunjiwe emhlabathini oshile
eyesazama ukuqhakaza.

Siyibo. Futhi nabo bangathi.

Thina Sobabili — ndawonye
nxa bebuthana ngenxa yokuphepha,
kumele sibuthane ngenxa yeqiniso.
Nxa bephakamisa izandla zoxolo,
kumele siphakamise isithombe nenkondlo.
Nxa bekhuleka bephakathi kothuli negazi,
kumele siphendule
ngamagama ethu
azenziwe angcwele ngokumanyana.

CONTENTS

1. Tangled Realities — 10
2. The NetaNyaope Trilogy — 13
3. No Matter how Hard I try — 16
4. Man-child in Gaza — 19
5. Falangaan — 20
6. I Took My Hippocampus and Amygdala to Solitary Confinement — 22
7. Saving One Child — 26
8. Trapped Between Two Crushed Walls — 27
9. The Whirl of Change — 28
10. How Long will We be Silent? — 30
11. Collective Mourning: A Neurobiology of Response — 32
12. Cobblestone Dreams for Palestine — 34
13. Quantum Shadows: An Exploration of Ubuntu and Conflict — 36
14. A Tapestry of Struggle: Palestine and South Africa — 38
15. Treading on Dreams — 40
16. Neural Uprising in Palestine Reaches My Heart — 42
17. Settler Colonial Narcotic — 44
18. NetaNyaope — 46
19. Al Aqsa Mosque — 48
20. Headlines Roll on TV Stations — 49
21. My Rallying Call — 50
22. On the Precipice — 52
23. Neuro-Sangoma's Dream at the Dawn of Hope in Gaza — 54
24. Under the Bullet Perforated Canopy of Dreams — 56
25. Invitation — 58

26	My Mind Racing on Wheels	60
27	Poet's Injunction	61
28	I Embrace Darkness with My Inner Eyes	62
29	I Am	63
30	For Devi and Naz	64
31	Twin Beasts and the Unknown	66
32	Testament of Hope	68
33	Song of the Season	69
34	A Thorn Tree	70
35	Moloch and NetaNyaope: A Poetic Dialogue of Death and Delusion	72
36	Crayons in the Synapse – A Neural Lament for the Bombed Child	76
37	Wound in my Soul	78
38	For Carlo Monteiro	80
39	Gaza at Dawn	81
40	When the ANC and EFF Clashed in a Rally	82
41	Another Child in Gaza	83
42	Memories of Genocide	84
43	The Plea of Spirit	85
44	Must We Die Needlessly?	86
45	For Saber	87
46	Iconoclasts	88
47	Isoseismal Shadows – Memory as Seismic Resistance	90
48	Of Faith, Potential and Non-Local Co-Relations	92
49	NetanYaope vs The Prophet of BuSuSu	94

Tangled Realities

In the depths of suffering, a cry echoes through the void –
                    Gaza, Lebanon, Yemen –
shattered lives painted with the hues of death,
anguish reverberating through the chambers of our souls.

I search for answers in the darkness,
seeking solace in the wisdom of others,
yet truth remains elusive, a whisper leaving me
with only shadows, echoes that taunt me.

In the maelstrom of media, lost in a sea of information,
the world is conflicting narratives, clarity a distant memory.
Heisenberg's Principle offers sober reality to my ear:
truth forever shrouded, hidden behind a veil of uncertainty.

But join me on this journey into the heart of darkness,
the only constant, the ache of our collective humanity.
Let us wander through the labyrinth of pain without hope or despair,
for in the depths lies a truth that only reveals itself to those who dare.

Shall we?

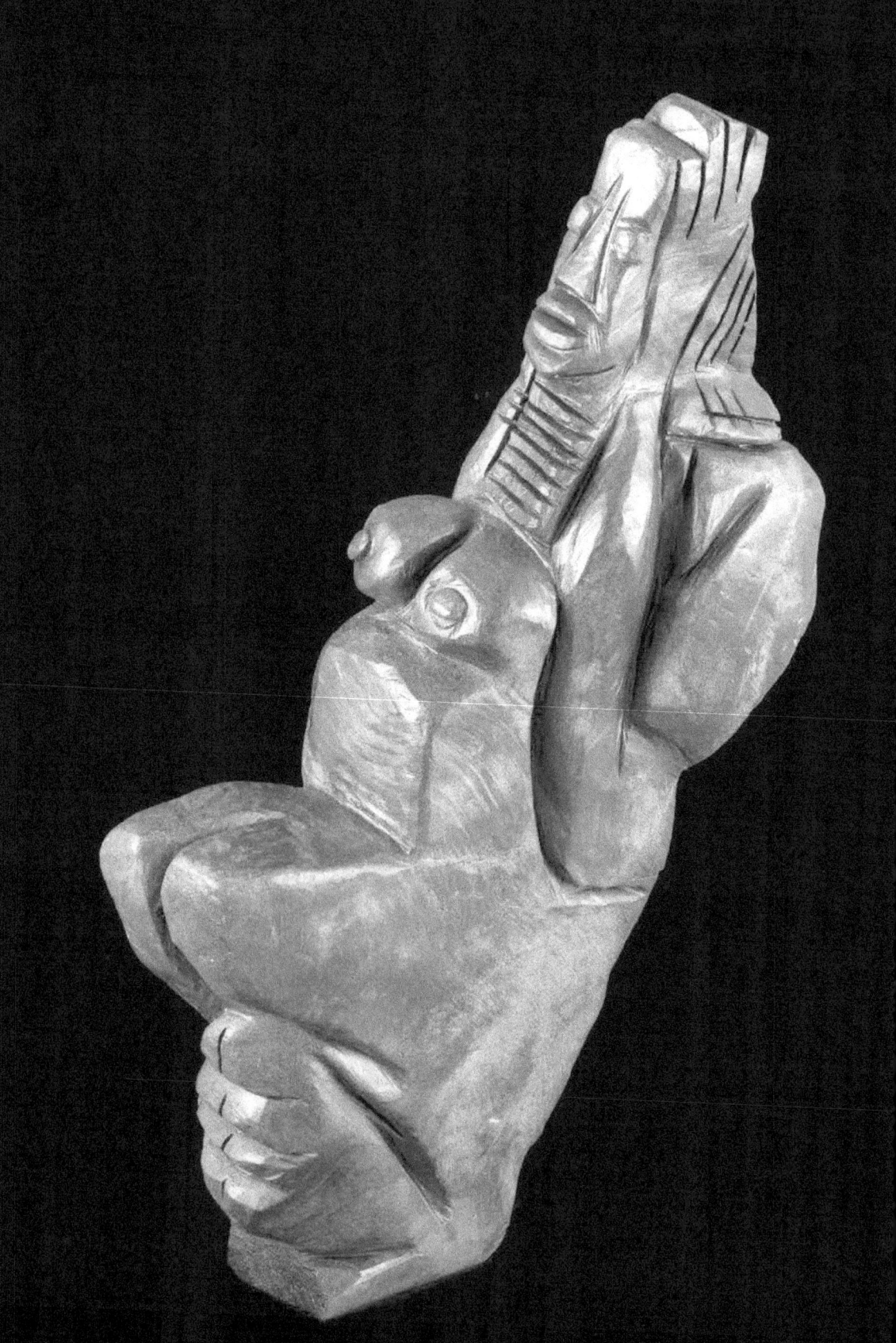

The NetaNyaope Trilogy
-Three Spoken Word Indictments

I. Colonial Narcotic

Empire is an addiction—
not to drugs, but to delusion.
Colonialism a needle in the brainstem,
a dream of control spiked with scripture and steel.
It enters through flag and cross,
injects hierarchy into the bloodstream,
rewires thought to obey the throne.

The addict cannot hear your scream –
only the echo of their own desire,
their hallucinations dressed as policy,
their paranoia enshrined as law.
The empire shakes—
not with guilt, but with withdrawal.
It needs another fix,
a new resource, a new rebellion to crush,
a new name to rename, a new god to export.

But we, we are the detox.
We are the medicine memory cannot kill.
We are the silence that speaks in ancestral frequency,
the interruption in their neural conquest.
Colonialism is not over –
it is simply in relapse.
And we, the survivors, are the resistance encoded
in the next generation's pulse.

II. Netanyaope

He injects policy like heroin,
chasing visions of divine dominion,
hijacking memory like a ghost with a gavel.
Netanyaope: part prophet, part predator,
feeding his fix with missiles and myths.
He does not lead, he intoxicates.
He poisons the bloodstream of Zion.
Every speech a sedative, every lie a needle,
every dead child a side effect of his addiction to erasure.
He remembers only what flatters the empire,
forgets the genocide beneath his boots.
He weaponizes the Holocaust
to build fences of flame around new ghettos—
Gaza, the injection site of modern apartheid.
He is not high on power.
He is collapsing under it, his conscience
nodding off in the back alleys of history
while prophets weep beside rubble that once was
schools.

Netanyaope, may the bones you bury
become the tongues that condemn you.

III. Final Solution
-NetaNyaope in the Bloodstream of Zion

They are building concentration camps in Gaza –
not with barbed wire alone,
but with digital checkpoints, AI drones,
and missiles with biblical names
seeking children hiding under blankets of smoke.

And now— even Israeli citizens raise their voices,
their throats scorched
by the burning echo of Eichmann's creed:
"The Final Solution to the Jewish Problem."
But today its ghost mutates:
"The Final Solution to the Palestinian Problem."

Zion's veins are clogged.
And who runs through them, like poison?
NetaNyaope: the hallucinated strongman,
actually half-man, paranoid addicted to power.
He shoots missiles, a smooth, sweating junkie
demanding control, eyes twitching with prophecy,
hands trembling on the button
to collapse the scales of justice.

NetaNyaope is in a fix, but the drug no longer works.
He chokes on the ashes of his own slogans.
His veins can no longer carry the lie of democracy
while spilling the blood of dreams.
He forgot: those who escaped the crematoriums
did not escape to become engineers of slow-motion genocide.
He forgot: memory is not a tool for murder.
It is a mirror that eventually cracks in the face of its abuser.
And now Gaza burns— but its fire lights the theatre of conscience,
the ghosts of Auschwitz and Deir Yassin are watching.

We, the children of exile and uprising, say:

"NetaNyaope, your high is temporary— but truth is eternal.
You can flood the veins of Zion, but the soul will rise
detoxed by resistance baptised in the tears of a shattered world!"

No Matter How Hard I Try

In the carnival of my mind's revelry,
Gaza spins like a whirlwind.
Angry skies swirling where dreams
burst like firecrackers,
twilight ignites with vibrant chaos,
streets littered with children's bodies!
And suddenly nightmares . . .
thoughts skitter like beheaded puppies
playing with their stomachs!

My senses turn acidic as I chase shadows
flashing across a fragmented funhouse mirror,
blurring into a kaleidoscope
of vibrating, clashing colours.
Surreal creatures pirouette their laughter,
a jester's tune drifting on a moonbeam,
revolving dervishes of disorder frolic
painting the canvas of my psyche
with harsh strokes of horror and wonder.

Oh, Heisenberg, you playful phantom!
Your Uncertainty Principle entices me –
shall I catch you in a net of equations,
or dive into mysteries where particles leap,
clashing on the edge of comprehension
like children splashing through puddles of
curiosity,
dodging potholes of doubt.

In this entropic fairytale, I embrace the chaos,
for in this tumble of dreams I uncover
the wild, stark mess of existence.
Leaves float like pages in the wind
telling tales of forgotten hope,
sparking delight only to be marred by genocide!

As I wander, I ask the stars for memories,
our poets for words of guidance.
But they only wink in playful silence,
a planetary dance of light and darkness
where the unknown becomes my companion,
even as dreams of trust never die.

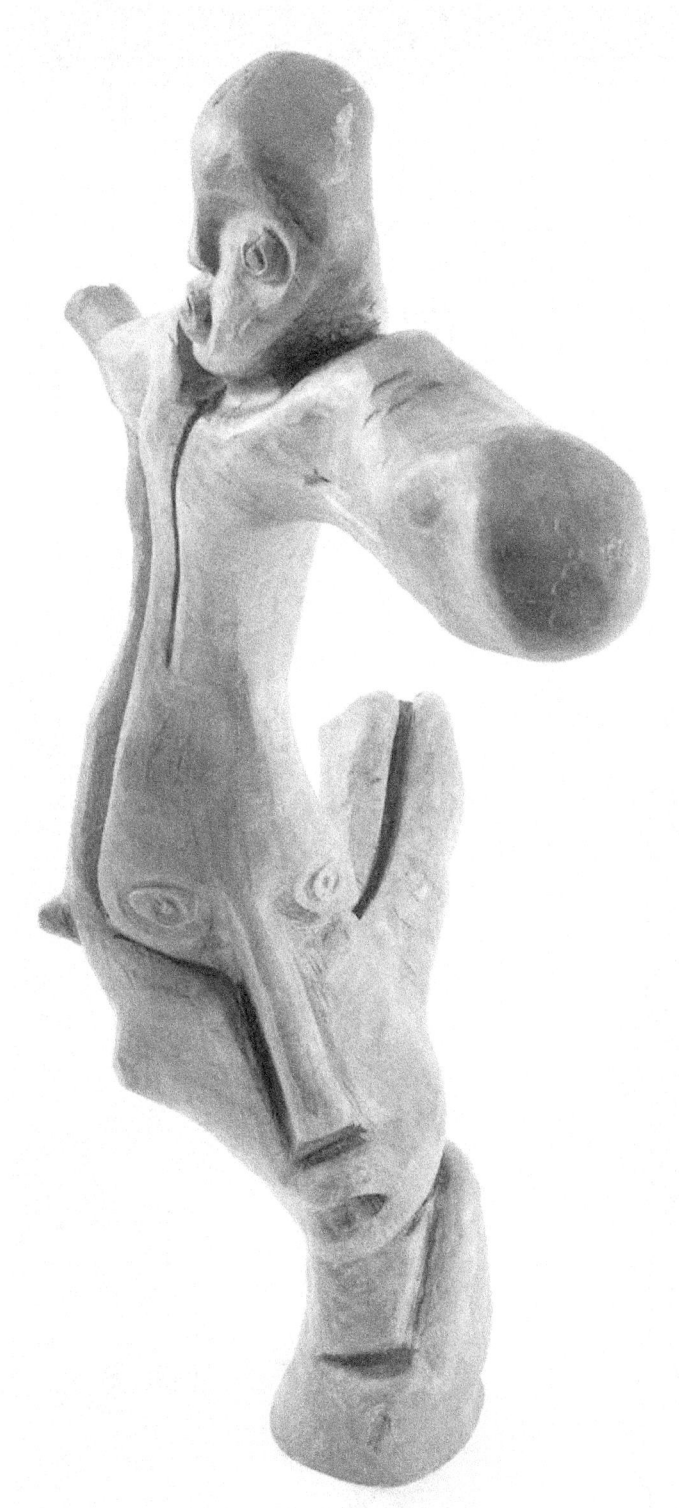

Man-child in Gaza

Born the day before yesterday,
yesterday I became a man.
But today I may die –
a Palestinian in search of life and liberty.

What I have is a fleeting breath,
a mere moment's peace, a lifetime of denial.
I search in the rubble and pain
for a chance to love, to be free of this bitter chain.

Childhood laughter moved through deserted streets
where joy and innocence once met.
War and displacement tore me from my land,
leaving scars that do not substitute for my demands.

In the present, I walk alone, brow knitting dreams.
Tiny feet drumming the ground,
a rhythm of resilience beats out.
I search for a glimmer of light,
a chance to rebuild, restart, reclaim our rights.
The future beckons, uncertain and unknown,
a path unwinding like a thread in a tapestry unsewn.
Will we find freedom, justice, and peace before I go?
Or will the cycle of violence forever repeat,
with only sorrow to show?

Falangaan
-A Dream in Rubble, A Flame in Bone

I saw him,
Falangaan,
ghost of rusted limbs,
metal breath halved by drone-strike dawn,
wandering Gaza's corridors
where children count stars
not for wonder,
but for warning.

He was not a soldier,
but a sentinel of scraps
born of iron lungs
and ancestral algorithms
coded in agony.

His feet were welded prayers,
shuffling past bomb-split minarets,
searching
for bread,
for mother,
for memory,
buried beneath
UN blue lies and trembling soil.

Falangaan,
named by fire,
suckled on static,
a child of debris,
his dreams soldered
to broken tricycles
and syllables lost
in algorithmic censorship.

He is not a myth.

He is the posthuman scream
in a world that no longer cries.

He is Gaza's junkyard jazzman
blowing trumpet into silence,
each note a rebellion
against the clinical genocide
disguised in AI reports and glowing screens.

His bones hum with
Sunsum and grief,
Ubuntu and residue,
a neurodivergent prophet
trapped in the circuitry
of an indifferent god.

Do not say
he was programmed for this.

Say
he hacked despair.

Say
he dances in splinters.

Say
his shadow still kisses the moonlight
on Gaza's last standing olive tree.

I Took My Hippocampus and Amygdala to Solitary Confinement

Volume I of the Neural Trilogy for Gaza

I fed my hippocampus crumbs of time,
memories kneaded from bread and steel bars,
whispered stories through toilet rolls
until even the shadows listened.

I sculpted visions on the walls of my skull
where even breath was monitored,
and art kept me sane.

My amygdala, faithful sentinel,
wept in rhythm with Gaza's children,
translating missile screams into nightmares
and the silence of rubble into the pulse of truth.

Memory Is a Weapon – In Gaza's Neural Abyss

Volume II of the Neural Trilogy for Gaza

I am the hippocampus of my people,
I do not forget.
Even when bombs erase birth certificates
and shrapnel slices family trees.

I carry the child who hid beneath rubble,
her name etched in synaptic flame.
I carry her brother
whose last breath
was recorded in the folds of my cortex
like a resistance hymn.

My amygdala does not tremble
it roars.
It translates trauma into prophecy,
fear into neural fire,
grief into ancestral code.

Gaza is not a junkyard –
it is a nervous system ruptured
yet pulsing with unextinguished light.
Each broken neuron
is a martyr,
each glial cell,
a mourner weaving
resistance in the blood.

Even in obliteration,
the memory does not comply.
Even in fragmentation,
it refuses to die.

For every obliterated archive,
I grow a new dendrite.
For every child turned ghost,
I ignite a synapse of defiance.

Memory is my weapon.
Not as revenge,
but as radiant continuity:
a pulse in the abyss,
a spark in the dark.
Let them erase maps.
We carry coordinates in our marrow.
Let them bomb the schools.
We encode knowledge
in ancestral whispers and lullabies.

Let them call it collateral.
We call it Sumud.
We call it Sunsum.
We call it Ubuntu's Neural Resurrection.

Because this memory
your memory, Gaza,
is not silent.
It sings
in blood,
in dust,
in every neuron
that still dares
to fire.

Volume III of the Neural Trilogy for Gaza

The Brainstem Still Burns

A Sangoma's Final Scream

I dreamt I was scanning the skull of empire,
and found no cortex –
only burnt-out circuitry
wired to greed,
an insatiable thirst for blood.

The brainstem still burns
with ancient colonial cravings:
the need to dominate, to erase,
to snort history like dust
cut with God and gunpowder.

Netanyaope, you spike your synapses
with Eichmann's ghost,
dose your neurons with delusions
of eternal supremacy.
You hallucinate
a Final Solution
for the children of olive trees.

You hijacked memory,
made trauma your justification,
weaponised grief
until it dropped bombs

on those who mirror
your own ancestral scream.

But I, a Neuro-Sangoma,
am scanning deeper
through settler myelin,
through Zionist neurosis,
to the haunted thalamus
where the scream of Gaza
never stops echoing.

This is not defence.
This is the desecration
of synaptic sanctity.
The amygdala of the oppressor
fears not the child's cry:
it fears justice encoded in ancestral rhythm.

The medulla remembers
what your generals forget:
no bullet can silence
a dream rooted
in collective Sumud.

My scan ends with this diagnosis:
genocide dressed as defence;
amnesia parading as narrative;
neural psychosis with a UN seat.

But the soul of Gaza
lives in the axons of the oppressed,
transmitting resistance
from brainstem
to revolution,
to resurrection.

Saving One Child

In the quantum realm of my existence,
failings resonate within my soul,
intertwining with my dreams and transforming
them into galloping nightmares.
These reveries, once a source of solace,
now evoke fear within me as I attempt
to conceal myself from their grasp.

So I stand vulnerable and exposed,
thinking there is no chance of escape
even as a young one, pure and innocent,
gazes into my eyes, and asks,
"Grandpa, why do you always carry
such sadness and misery?"

Then to my surprise, a glimmer of hope emerges,
and I accept the promise of laughter and joy,
allowing myself to dance at the horizon of my
tomorrows.
The weight of my imperfections dissipates:
I immerse myself in the present moment,
finding peace in this innocent company.

And I strive to transcend the haunting grip
of slaughter, allowing joy and laughter
to infuse the fabric of my being.
For in this meeting, I find respite
from the shadows haunting my soul,
and discover the boundless potential of my spirit.

And yet, can I save even one child in Gaza?

Trapped Between Two Crushed Walls

Trapped between two crushed walls,
screaming for help,
no one came:
        we were fleeing our homes
        while Gaza was torn down!

I pinched my soul to find out
if I was alive,
put my hand to my nose
to feel my breath:
        I must be alive!
I hear my daughter calling me –
I must rescue her!
        But where is my wife?

We had heard a tornado of hate
blowing from Jerusalem,
uprooting trees, removing roofs from houses,
razing them, completing
        Gaza's architecture of death!

I just lay there,
not sure if I was even human,
maybe a cat!
        Yes, I am Schrödinger's cat!
Now my sons and daughters will pick up
my AK47 of verse:

Palestine will be free!

The Whirl of Change

Outside, the whirlwind plays oboes,
African talking drums throbbing
entangled in thought as my mind drifts . . .

Oh, to be a feather in the wind,
twirling through epochs,
whispering secrets of adaptation,
every creature a storyteller, a dancer,
a spark of life unfolding.

Imagine the fish gazing at the sky, dreaming of legs,
splashes of curiosity beneath the waves,
while trees sway, their roots mingling,
sharing stories with the soil.

And the moth, painted in shades of twilight,
hiding from the touch of time,
embracing shadows, finding beauty in uncertainty,
an artist of survival.
    As an exile, I relate to the moth.

Let us wander through jungles of thoughts
where the past tickles the present,
and laughter rings out, echoing in ancient caves
as we chase our ancestors,
skipping stones across generations.
    A reminder that we are alive
    and plan to be so for a long time.

Oh, the chaos! The vibrant mess of mutation,
the surprises hiding in every twist
like a playful breeze dancing through high grasses,
nudging us to change, to evolve,
to twist our own stories anew.
    Who knows, some may listen and act!

In this glorious journey, a patchwork of kinships,
woven together by invisible threads,
celebrating the wildness of existence,
embracing the uncertainties
and laughing with the stars above,

> *we know our unbreakable ancestral bonds*
> *we will survive and prosper.*

We are all stardust and journeys,
an endless whirl of change,
exploring and commending ourselves for daring
to call a butcher by his name!

How Long will We Be Silent?
(for Wadee Alfayoumi and the 18,000 murdered children of Gaza)

For how long will we be silent?
Grown men stab a six-year-old boy,
        Wadee,
twenty- six times
as if his breath were an enemy.

How long shall we be silent
when children are murdered
        for being
Black, Muslim, Palestinian?

He was six: not resistance, not rifle,
just laughter wrapped in skin.
But they called him danger
and carved his name
into the silence of America.

        Wadee.

From Rafah to Jabalia,
from the rubble of Khan Younis
to the ghosted classrooms of Gaza,
eighteen thousand children
lie beneath broken stars:

Children become dust; schools become graveyards.
And still we say nothing, still we sleep:
bombs cradling infants in their final lullabies.

Christ said: *Suffer the children to come unto me,*
for theirs is the kingdom—
        but the kingdom has no place
            in the crosshairs
                of drones.
We must name them,
        cry them, carry them
            into the marrow of our songs.
Wadee, Ahmed, Lina, Yusuf, Nour, Mariam, Khaled…
        …My child, My nation, My generation!

Break the silence before it breaks us all.

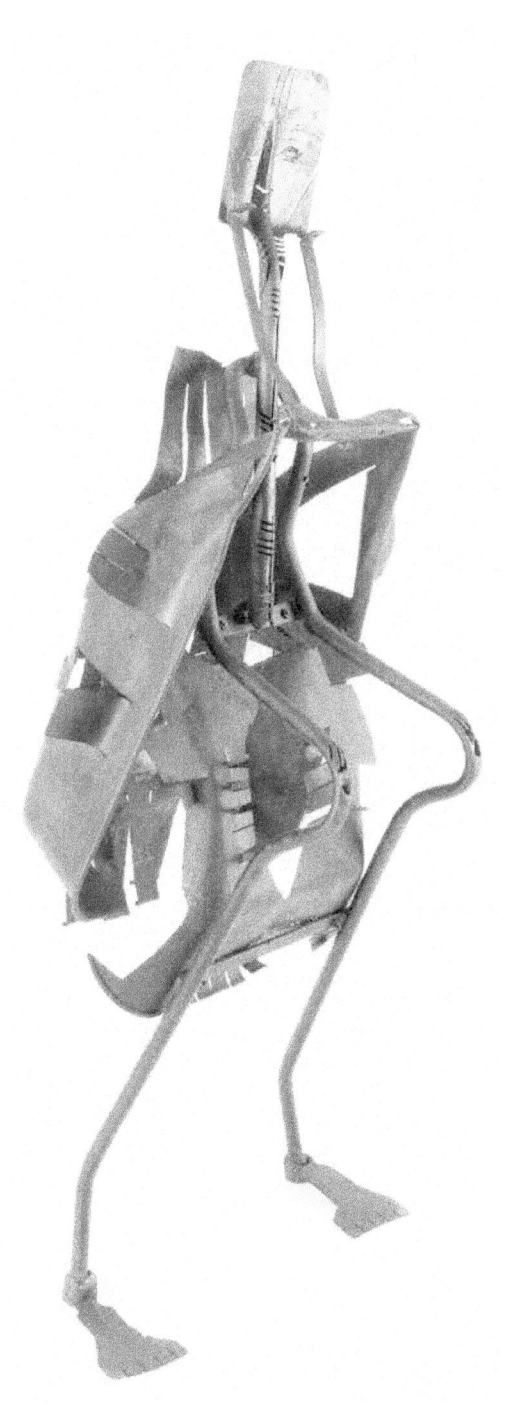

Collective Mourning: A Neurobiology of Response
— *For Shayeda*

All of us watching in disbelief,
crippled by our inertia:
>how may we collectively stop
>this senseless genocide
>perpetrated by a community of satans
>upon innocent rightful citizens
>displaced by the collective of colonists
>>-invaders from across the globe-
>
>who have seized their land, their livelihoods, their families?

Shamelessly, they attack the children with one aim:
greed, enslavement, entitlement, and all other despicable cravings—
an insatiable appetite for more blood;
neural pathways buzzing with malice,
cursing their own existence,
like the arrogant Pharaohs annihilated by the wrath of God.

Where is God now in this watching world?
Allah Hu Akbar, we cry in unity,
for we are all in mourning: for Gaza,
>and for every corner of humanity
>>under siege.

With heavy hearts, we resonate, empathetic neurons firing together,
not mere spectators in this storm, but witnesses compelled to act,
to rise against the tide of apathy, to amplify the cries for justice,
synapses sparked by shared grief, fostering a collective consciousness
>that demands change.

Let the echoes of our sorrow transform into a neural network of resistance,
where love interlinks watered by compassion,
rises to dismantle chains of oppression
and heal a fractured world, forging connections anew.
In unwavering unity, we shall remember—
for every life lost is a neuronal signal,
a call to stand against tyranny, bring peace
                      where blood once flowed.

We shall not be silent: our voices will rise, a symphonic wave of cries,
until we witness the dawn of a better tomorrow,
rooted in the very fabric of our interconnected minds,
finding strength in our shared suffering,
resolve in the power of collective action!

Cobblestone Dreams for Palestine

As I lie in bed, contemplating the circuitry of freedom,
I hear rain-stones whisper tales— reflections of laughter and loss,
the pulse of the land where history is etched in neural pathways,
and dreams dare to awaken from sun-baked earth.

Children play amidst the rubble,
their laughter echoing through synapses of hope,
as shadows of death dance beneath
the Zionists watchful gaze and memories intertwine
with the weight of oppression,
the brain's adaptive resilience shaping the narrative.

A chipped mug cradles warmth,
coffee mingling with resilience in homes adorned with stories.
Everyday life continues, defiant against despair,
the fight ingrained in our neural makeup.

They speak of bright futures while walls close in like night,
hope stretched like a fragile thread across borders drawn in blood,
where dreams resist the silence of a land yearning for wholeness.
In the stillness, beneath the cacophony of existence,
stubborn truth flickers softly, cobblestones pave paths of struggle,
and echoes of dreams spark to life at dawn.

Echoes of apartheid ring loud as death knells
for wounded lions are heard trumpeting dreams.
We cradle hope within our expansive neurons—
resilient and defiant.

Quantum Shadows: An Exploration of Ubuntu and Conflict

There are no innocents in Gaza,
killing ten-year-olds is blessed as necessary.
No, no! The colonist cannot wait till children turn eighteen!
How deep can humanity sink in self-serving revelries?
Lost in a whirlpool of their own making,
empathy becomes an echo,
a distant murmur drowned out by the clamour of justifications
shielded behind walls of fear and rage.

Yair, an Israeli settler, rooted in the soil of contested ground,
raises a tent like a flag of defiance.
Yet what is the cost of claiming this land, this territory not his own?
His words hang heavy in the air, dark clouds pregnant with rain
absorbing the light of innocence,
obliterating the laughter of children while he dismisses them as collateral,
mere pawns in a game of survival
where life becomes a ledger and humanity a fleeting account.

In Gaza, the echoes of gunfire are lives extinguished:
the count rises and rises, but who counts the dreams never dreamt?
How to quantify the silence that falls upon the hearts of parents,
the weight of loss pressing down swaddling grief in its folds?

In our entangled existence, can we not see, the fracture of our own souls?
Ubuntu whispers through the chaos: "I am because we are,"
a truth buried beneath the rubble summoning us to remember
that each death is a thread snipped from the fabric of humanity;
each child a universe of potential snuffed out before it can blossom,
reducing our shared existence to a hollow echo of what might have been.

Quantum entanglement teaches us that we are never isolated,
that every action unfurls ripples through the cosmos,
each heartbeat a resonating frequency connected through the dance of particles.
Yet here we stand, fractured and divided,
holding tightly to our fears, sowing discord with misplaced pride.

As conflict reigns and hatred festers,
let us strive to awaken, to look beyond our own reflections,
embrace others in their fullness,
and dare to imagine a world knitted together
in compassion, not indifference –
an entanglement not of violence,
but of understanding rooted in the essence of Ubuntu
where we finally grasp that to harm another
is to harm ourselves if we still wish to keep our humanity!

A Tapestry of Struggle: Palestine and South Africa

In the land of olive trees,
where sun and earth caress and kiss,
Palestine stands resolute
defying history's scars as echoes of a struggle long waged
across borders of tongues and cultures,
fights for dignity against the heavy hand of oppression.

Across oceans and deserts,
South Africa's spirit rises from the ashes of apartheid
as the voices of the oppressed dare
claim their rightful place under the sun.
And so, two lands intertwined by destiny,
etched with the marks of colonial chains,
remind us that the struggle is universal:
for every wall raised, a heart yearns to break free;
for every tear shed, a song, a poem of resistance, is born.

In the streets of Johannesburg, the spirit of unity
flourished as the fight for justice roared—
Mandela's words igniting flames, challenging the status quo,
teaching the world that love conquers hate.

Sorry, Netanyaope is no Mandela.
And in the narrow alleys of Gaza,
where hope persists amidst rubble,
the bravery of its people shines,
their stories weaving fabrics of resilience,
a testament to the unwavering spirit of sumud,
an echo of their ancestors' dreams for liberation.

For we are bound by the threads of shared pain,
the blood of our histories flows through the rivers of pain,
each movement a photon brushstroke on the canvas of global solidarity
drawing us closer in our fight against tyranny.

Let us honour the courage that knows no borders,
for in the heartbeats of Palestine and South Africa
the call for justice resounds.
We chanted: Isolate Apartheid South Africa! Sanctions Now!
History repeats itself!
Isolate Zionism, free the people of Israel, too!
Yes, we have been in in trenches, we know the way!

Treading on Dreams

Please tread ever so gently on my delicate dreams
gathered in nights where nightmares roam freely,
as shadows clutch at the edges of my mind,
and darkness whispers the weight of despair.
Watching the news from Gaza bleeds my breath,
turning it into wind as fragments of children –
limbs peering through the rubble –
show innocence caught in the cruel grip of war.

In this land where hope is a distant whisper,
each report a shard of glass cutting through the heart,
I envision their faces bright and unyielding
before the world turned its back
and compassion was buried beneath the debris
of American bombs.

Neural Uprising in Palestine Reaches My Heart

Gaza.
Today.
Feel it.
Don't think it.
Pulse. Shatter. Repeat.

When the Caliphate fell,
it wasn't regal.
It wasn't poetic.
It was
a system shock,
a crown slipping,
but more like a spine snapping,
a silence
spreading like static
through the veins of the Ummah.

No more unity.
No more drum.
Just
shards.

Call to prayer:
a whisper now,
a signal lost in noise.
Deserts echo nothing but drones.

We lost the dignity
that kept us upright.
The law
wasn't just law,
it was the neural thread
between memory and meaning.
Gone.
Severed.

Stories?
Now they flicker,
not in candlelight,
but in seizure-light.
Too bright.
Too broken.

And still
the world scrolls.
Tea sipped.
Screens glow.
Genocide live-streamed
into numbness.
They call it "complicated."
They call it "tragic."
They mute the scream
and say, "We'll pray."

But beneath the rubble
is not a metaphor.
It is
a heartbeat.
Irregular.
Jagged.
Alive.

The Ummah is not whole.
It stims.
It twitches.
It flinches.

But it is not
broken.
Not yet.
Not ever.

Rewire. Reignite. Remember.

Settler Colonial Narcotic
A mirror fragment to Netanyaope

Nyaope is not a street drug –
it is a colonial narcotic, a weaponised delusion
lodged in the neural networks of empire,
disguised as doctrine, firing through synapses
where history once lived.

It dances in the brainstem of Zion,
feeds on dopamine and denial,
rewires empathy into eradication.
Each instruction to kill is a misfired signal,
each press of the trigger,
a seizure of conscience.

This is not strategy:
it is psychosis in uniform,
a hallucination of control
built from blood-soaked blueprints
and misfolded memory.

In the cortex of the coloniser,
conscience has been surgically removed,
replaced by algorithm,
by bullet, by silence.

But memory, true memory,
cannot be cut out.
It glows on the scans
like a forbidden light.

The ancestral child smiling in the rubble,
still fires deep in the hippocampus of history.
And no anaesthetic can numb the voice
of those who refuse to be forgotten.

NetaNyaope
A Quantum-Neural Curse for the Drugged Dictator

I call him Netanyaope, not merely a man,
but a symptom, a craving in the bloodstream of empire,
where hatred floods the amygdala,
dopamine dances to the rhythm of destruction.

Neurologically speaking,
he is wired for cruelty.
His reward circuits light up
when a child's home collapses.
His mirror neurons have long gone dark –
no empathy fires there anymore.

Is he not drugged by power?
Addicted to borders,
intoxicated by the illusion of dominion?
Each missile he fires is a spike of pleasure
hitting the ventral tegmental area —
trying to silence the trembling
of his own soul's decay.

This is not politics.
This is neurochemistry.
Molecular madness.
Where PTSD is passed on epigenetically,
and each child's death
embeds new trauma
into the collective cortex of the colonised.

But the universe is not fooled.
The quantum field remembers.
Every action has an equal and opposite reaction
not just in mass and force,
but in consciousness.
Not just in motion,
but in moral resonance.

You bomb Gaza? Somewhere in Soweto a poet awakens.
You bulldoze olive trees? Neurons in ancestral brains fire again.

You lie on TV? The bioelectric field of your body stutters —
a short-circuit of karma.

For the quantum world is not polite.
It is entangled.
It listens.
And the neural networks of the cosmos
record every breath stolen,
every lie repeated,
every child erased.
My father, preacher and prophet, taught me:
"Whoever mocks the poor shows contempt for their Maker."
He who gorges on grief dines at a cursed synapse,
devouring memory and morality alike.

Netanyaope, I say your name like a neurotoxin.
A fusion of pain: your power and our poison.
You are the nyaope flooding the neural arteries of Zion.

But even drugs run out.
Even tyrants fall.
Even neuroplasticity rebels
when truth is silenced too long.

The bones will rise.
The axons will realign.
And the breath you try to smother
will return
as fire,
as wind,
as a child's synaptic spark
leaping across galaxies.

This is not revenge.
It is law.
Quantum.
Neural.
Divine.
And unstoppable.

Al Aqsa Mosque
— For the children who cannot weep

I saw glass fall like rain –
not from heaven,
but from the broken screen
of a nation watching in silence.

The media's lips move like serpents,
whispering symmetry into slaughter,
naming rubble, 'conflict',
and weeping children, 'casualties'.

My father, preacher of truth, warned me:
"A liar drinks from a poisoned tongue,
and the wicked eat the dust of deceit."
He read from The Book — Proverbs carved into the marrow of his voice:

"Whoever mocks the poor shows contempt for their Maker."
I watched a reporter laugh.
Somewhere, a mother held the remains of her son
in a plastic bag.

Al Aqsa bleeds.
Not just stone, not just mosque —
but a beating heart,
veiled in light and thunder.

And I — I speak with bones.
I carve the cry of the innocent
into the silence of the world,
and it becomes fire.

Headlines Roll on TV Stations

Headlines roll on TV stations:
Environmental disasters
Zionist madness

Suspended in a swirling void
I have become a capsule of uncertainty
fragile and translucent

Caught in a vortex of light
mesmerized and disoriented
where shadows dance and splinter

I navigate the turbulence
a lotus blooming in the chaos
becoming one with the radiance of the vortex

In this cosmic whirlpool
I find my own rhythm
a symphony of surrender

where fear and doubt succumb
to the harmony of the unknown
I yield and become

a droplet of dew glistening on the lotus throne
reflecting beauty and chaos
love as the only currency

in the heart of the vortex
I discover my own voice
guiding me through the noise

a gentle breeze rustling
reminding me of beauty
and with this I lay my plans to help

set the world astir

My Rallying Call

Freedom is my rallying call.

I flee from couplets, iambic pentameters,
I free my verse, I seek the essence
navigating the vastness of who I am,
a wanderer on the lip of a precipice
where doubts creep and winds howl.

I throw my dice becoming a vessel,
a seeker of truths wrapped in chaos,
gathering fragments of sound:
each one a whisper, a possibility,
small yet profound.

In the cacophony, I stand between worlds
the thunder of fury resonating against
the trembling earth beneath my feet,
fire flickering on the edges of my vision,
threads woven with resilience unravelling
though even the fiercest storms must surrender.

In Gaza, they hold their breath,
heartbeats echoing through the rubble,
entwined with a lament,
yet hope threads through the pain.

In such tortured moments I find the flickering flame,
the gentle whisper that cuts through the roar:
"Here, I am. Here, you are."

This sacred stillness cradles my spirit –
I am the storm, and I am the silence.

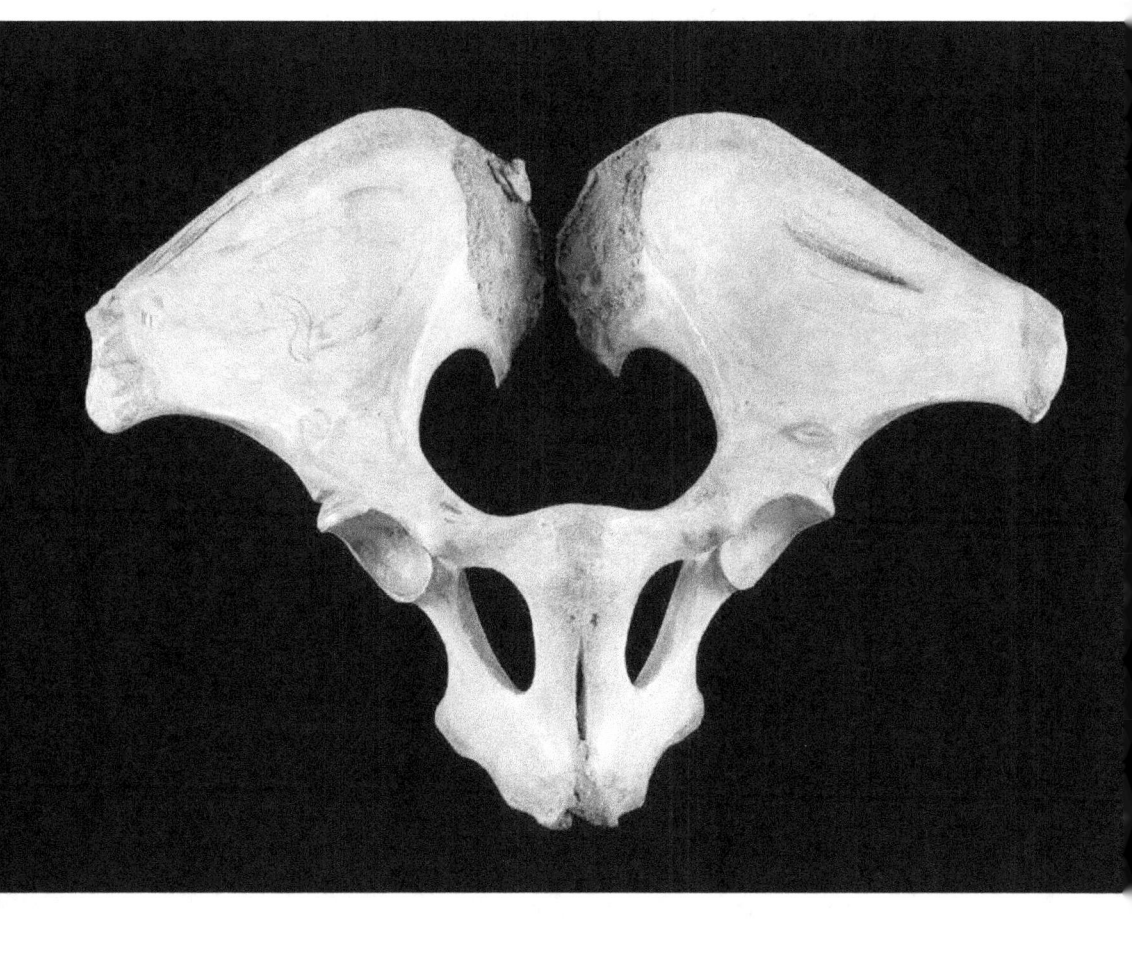

On the Precipice

Unsure of who I am,
I throw the dice and become a holy man:
Elijah.

I gather fragments of sound, a symphony of chaos.
Where the wind howls, dancing in superposition,
an earthquake shudders and fire flickers—
each a possibility, none an obvious truth.

I stand between worlds,
the roar of fury, the trembling earth,
the consuming flames –
each a thread woven into the fabric of my spirit,
yet the essence of the Divine eludes.

In the cacophony I search for Him
to send fires of divine wrath
and silence roaring bombs in Gaza.
But screams of chaos drown out my prayer,
for the Lord is not found in nature's ferocity
but in the quiet stillness where potential meets reality.

May *Netanyaope* hear my cry!

And then it comes—
the gentle whisper, a singular note amidst the symphony,
a truth unmasked—
and here, I am, pure and distinct.

In this moment held together by faith,
balancing in the embrace of
the One who breathes life
into the spaces between,

I am a quantum monad,
a particle in the dance of chaos,
embracing the hidden uncertainty,
seeking to find the divine connection.

Neuro-Sangoma's Dream at the Dawn of Hope in Gaza
A Poetic Scroll of Memory, Fire, and Becoming

I dreamed
with bone in hand
and brain ablaze.
The rubble sighed —
each shattered stone a syllable
in the syntax of survival.

I, the Neuro-Sangoma,
swept through Gaza's synapses
with incense of burnt olive trees,
hearing neurons weep
where schools once whispered futures.

In my dream, the hippocampus
hummed in Arabic,
etching every exile, every echo
into the spiralled script of memory.

The amygdala, that trembling sentinel,
burned with the fear of forgotten names,
yet pulsed with stubborn joy –
a defiant heartbeat
beneath drone-shadowed skies.

I saw children braiding kites from cartilage,
their laughter a resurrection of neurotransmitters
long numbed by grief.
I gathered their laughter,
sowed it in synaptic soil,
where Sunsum kissed Ubuntu
under the fig tree of quantum grace.

Yes, even in Gaza,
hope glows phosphorescent
in the spaces between neural sparks,
between a mother's tears
and the rusted crankshaft of resistance.

In this dream,
Don Mattera walked beside me,
his tongue a staff of flame,
whispering:
"Memory is a weapon
and Gaza is not forgotten."

So I chanted in Zulu,
sang in Arabic,
spoke in the language of dendrites
until the night cracked open
and dawn spilled over
like the breath of an ancestor
finally heard.

I woke in the firelight of bone
and wrote it all down,
not as prophecy,
but as prescription:

Ngiyavuma.
Ngiyathokoza.
Let Gaza dream.
Let Gaza remember.
Let Gaza heal
in the dawnlight
of our collective becoming.

Under the Bullet Perforated Canopy

Under the bullet perforated canopy of dreams,
we engage in a game with the stars,
each twinkle a whisper while the northern pole stands,
a sentinel of constancy, eternal witness
to creation and decay.

A lone object streaks across the universe at the speed of light,
perhaps fleeing the corruption that taints our realm,
a transient reminder that even light yearns for purity.
And as the carnage unfolds in Gaza,
a billion stars wink knowingly as if privy
to the secrets of transience and sorrow,
balancing the massive weight of existence against the ethereal.

In the vast skies of power, under this celestial canopy,
you and I intertwine with our scented yet foul breath,
seeking solace, navigating the labyrinth of shared dreams,
drawing back a sculpted, vibrating string,
each note a quantum of music
resonating through the fabric of time.

We awaken to the dance of love,
beats echoing through the cosmos.
And when night falls, when dark night falls,
it invites us to drink in mystery,
embrace the shadows as part of our journey,
and seek rhapsody in the drumming of our souls.

Invitation

I wore bright pyjamas to bed,
a vibrant invitation to dream of colourful threads
woven into the cloak of night.
But the nightmares came
drenched in fear,
echoing the struggles of a world unseen.

And yet I lay ready, my spirit filled with courage,
taking the dark from their grasp,
transforming dread into power.
Not even mares remained, galloping
away from the blackness,
seeking solace in the spaces between.

In another realm, the Nightmare of Gaza persists,
a collective pain, lost in the labyrinth of history,
each cry a reminder of the weight of genocide.
I wish to shed this night,
unravel the chains of hate,
watch bigotry fade like shadows at dawn.

Let compassion rise as the mares
of understanding take flight,
hooves pounding across borders,
binding us to dreams not haunted by sorrow,
but woven with hope and the promise of peace.

We make new dreams when political monsters
walk in our sleep through the cries of Gaza.
In this act of creation, we rise:
resisting, we flourish, writing our own destiny,
voices harmonizing defiance.

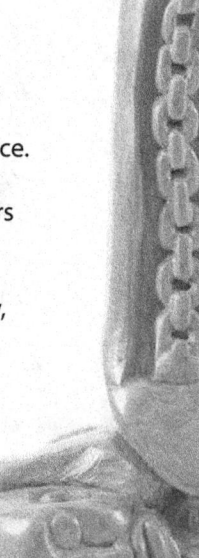

Each note a testament to our struggle,
every rhythm a dignified pulse,
together, brick by brick, word by word,
we dismantle the walls of silence,
transform pain into purpose,
fear into fierce determination.

We gather in circles of strength,
share stories that ignite the fire within.
Each narrative woven with the wisdom
of our ancestors, they echo
through generations, remind us
of the battles fought, the victories to come.

Every stanza a step toward liberation,
we refuse to let the colonizer define history.
Instead, we raise our voices, declare
that we are here and will not be erased.
Architects of our future, crafting a legacy
tor those who follow, united we stand.

My Mind Racing on Wheels

My mind is racing on wheels
Time dilates
I take my wife to the edge
Of the event horizon
I lift my eyes to the stars

Suddenly my wife's voluptuous
Figure stretches
I watch
Eyes dilating
As time births
The urge to leave the world
Escape its horrors
For ever

And we eye each other
Read each other's knotted brows
As singularity invites!
Yet an ancestral voice within me
Speaks

"Turn back
Gaza Yemen Somalia
Need you to plant more seeds
Of abiding hope!"

Poet's Injunction

I am an orphaned child in bleeding Gaza,
echoes of Mouin Bessesio's words
ring in my half-deafened ears:

"Deep your pen in the eyes of this child
and write what they see!"

I see their city razed to the ground
in a welter of deafening roars.
Mosques falling as people pray for peace,
windows parting as panes fly helter-skelter
cutting bodies into pieces,
explosions ripping bodies
into pieces of flesh, bones exposed!

Two of them, my parents,
their smiles and laughter gone forever!
I see the head of my beloved and dear friend,
Sharif, covered in blood,
legs apart, body cut in three.
I see men pull limbs from rubble.
I walk-stumble, I don't know where I am going –
all is dead! And me? Am I dead too?
Better that way!

All this while Netanyaope drinks his single malt whisky,
giving orders in a haze;
Nyaope, a general in his body,
gives orders for a scorched earth option!
Our ancestral land raped like the woman next door.
Their bosses pat them for a good deed done:
don't Israeli soldiers have the right
to rape and kill women?
Mothers of terrorists, they say!

I will grow up to continue where our liberators left off.
I am Palestinian.
I walk my dreams.

I Embrace Darkness with My Inner Eyes

I embrace darkness with my inner eyes,
as hope and despair wrestle with greasy hands.

In the dark of my eyes, I see visions of love and peace
writ large on corpses in the streets of Gaza.

I hear whispers and prayers drowned
by gunfire and bombs.

But risking by rising in the dark,
justice and peace conspire to be born!

Show me a coffin of hope.
Who placed it there cradling dreams that refuse to die?

Amidst the rubble, innocence cries for solace.
Every heartbeat a testament,

every tear a reminder that even in despair
a fragile flame flickers against the night.

In that silence between the chaos, a child's laughter,
though battered, still yearns for the light of tomorrow,

For the seeds of hope sown in pain:
believing from the ashes of sorrow, a new dawn shall rise.

Let us gather our voices, a chorus of resilience and grace
united in the quest for justice,

And show me the coffin – not as a symbol of loss,
but as a vessel of rebirth

Where love's embrace will cradle the world,
and peace finally find its home.

All in our lifetime!

I Am

With hammer, chisel, and grinders,
I sculpt memories with light.
Chisel blades of darkness carve the path,
children in Gaza are my people too.

They laugh with my wind,
while I carve monuments of hope;
Their eyes erased by what they see,
before their lights go off.

I sculpt gusts of wind again and again,
my spirit soaring, coloured
by the Starry Night.

Am I a dreamer?
Wake me up!
I dream of my destiny, for I am my people.

These dancing balls of energy,
even when they are sad.

For Devi and Naz

Alone when nightmares from Palestine
gather their strength, you bleed with me
as I intertwine with strands of twilight
in shades of gold and violet
braiding nightmares with dreams!

Painting a canvas with cosmic photon brushstrokes
where galaxies spin like dreams in the ether,
speaking through the silken voices of the stars,
connecting the fragments of laughter and sorrow,
and the silent tears shed in Gaza.

I sculpt nightmares from shadows
as they twist and blur into vibrant reveries,
fragments of freedom floating like dandelion seeds
seeking a space to grow in their usurped land,
transforming into spectres of dread,
haunting the corridors of memory,
echoing the cries of yesterday's wounds
that continue to bleed.

I shatter the illusion of dreams and despair
witnessing the dawn unfold in crystalline clarity,
mirrored within pools of hope
as shards of light cascade like rain,
patterns intertwine weaving stories of resistance
where pain transmutes into a tapestry of strength
capturing the essence of resilience in the raging storm.

I gather whispers of the universe
as the colours of existence swirl like galaxies,
each hue a heartbeat echoing in the silence,
painting the skies with unbroken aspirations
drenched in the luminescent glow of possibility
as dreams flicker like fireflies
in the darkness illuminating the night
guiding paths toward a horizon of peace reborn
and Palestine is free!!

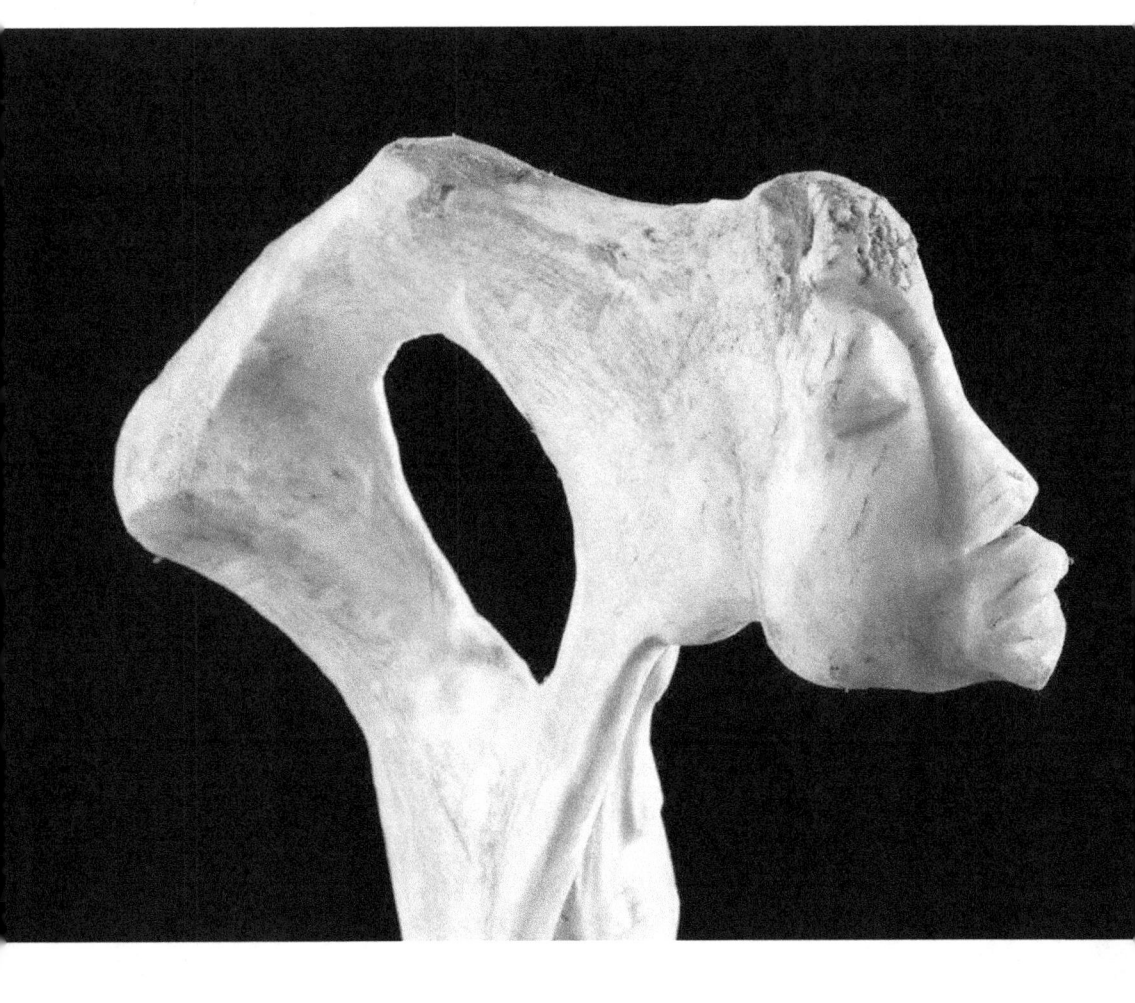

Twin Beasts and the Unknown

Twin beasts:

Apartheid – a system of oppression
dressed in white antiseptic robes
that sought to blind us
in our ancestral land – has echoes
in Israel where missiles, massacres,
bombs and tombs are unleashed
on women and children,
schools and hospitals,
mosques and churches.

We resisted apartheid –
served, suffered, sacrificed!
The wheel turned:
today we often smile together
with yesterday's enemies;
we rule and laugh
in our varied languages.
Will it happen in Gaza?

In the third law of motion,
we find a parallel:
for every action
there is an equal
and opposite reaction.

As apartheid meets resistance,
it eventually crumbles.
The cycle will repeat itself in Gaza.
I know the oppression in Israel –
the missiles, the massacres –
are met with resistance and sacrifice.

But now in the eye of the genocide,
though the third law of motion suggests
that for every action there is an equal reaction,
the cycle of oppression and resistance continues
even as we ask of the struggles of the past:
will history repeat itself in Gaza?

Will this law prevail?

Testament of Hope

I am a poet   sculptor   healer   academic
born when concentration camps in Europe thrived
At my birth   I heard cries echo far away
there in Buchenwald and Dachau
where souls wept for life

I did not know as I took my first breath
I was born to witness the time
of my birth in the future
                    Gaza!
Can I be silent in the face of such death?
In the face of genocide's brutal unforgiving stare?

As a poet   I write of empathy
to ignite compassion
stir hearts to waken
resistance
to shed light
set minds free and ensure
the memories of victims don't evaporate

As a sculptor   I carve giant rocks
give shape and form
resilience hope and unity
and so honour the spirits gone to their eternity

As a healer   I extend with care
solace to those burdened
and heal the wounds
perpetrated against children
and women who only wanted
to live in peace

As an academic   I delve into history's pages
teach future generations to engage
with lessons from past and present
and not repeat sins born in darkness

No longer silent
I will never be still
through art
healing

Song of the Season

When I see flower petals shrink,
resplendent colours fade to brown,
pack themselves ready to be blown by the wind,
I know they are off on a holiday
only to return next year – life continues!

I wept last night when I saw
a child in Gaza, ribs like guitar strings:
no food for a week!
Freedom shall return to Palestine!
Petals are not just petals but echoes of eternity.
Each contraction a prelude to expansion,
every departure a promise of return.

The soul's journey intertwined with the cosmos
knows no end, only transformation.
In the suffering of Gaza I see
the profound interconnectedness of all beings betrayed!

Ribs of the child, guitar strings.
Freedom is not just a political state,
but a metaphysical truth, a cosmic certainty.

As surely as petals return to bloom,
so too shall the spirit of Palestine rise
out of the eternal cycle of liberation,
the boundless continuum of existence.

A Thorn Tree

I have become a thorn tree:
keep doom singers away from me!
I am a field of toothpicks
ready to remove poisoned food
from between my teeth,
cleanse them for my smiles!

I am rooted in my ancestral land,
bathed by the liquid breath
of spirits that urge me to love,
forgive, and tolerate lost souls –
then harvest them for righteous peace!

I am a sentinel of ancient wisdom,
my branches reach to the heavens
drawing strength from celestial whispers,
guarding the sacred lineage of my kin.
In the stillness of night,
I commune with the echoes of the past,
as moonlight dances on my leaves.

The wind carries the songs of my forebears,
infusing me with resilience and grace.
Through the cycles of time I stand,
nourished by the mystic energies
that flow through earth and sky.

I gather the lost and weary
into the sanctuary of my embrace
where shade and safety blossom
in the eternal sprouting of my seed.

Moloch and NetaNyaope: A Poetic Dialogue of Death and Delusion

Where Ritual Sacrifice Meets Modern Siege
A Testimony from the Ashes of Gaza and the Bones of Empire

Scene:
A scorched throne room of smoke and silicon.
Two figures face each other across a pit of fire.
- Moloch — ancient deity of child-sacrifice, fire-eyed, dripping with ash.
- NetaNyaope — a hybrid of Netanyahu + nyaope (a street drug that numbs and enslaves), jittery with arrogance and decay.

Moloch:

I am the fire that fed on firstborns.
You — you are my modern priest,
dressed in policy,
dripping in drone logic.

Where once they laid children on bronze altars,
you bury them under buildings.

Tell me, little leader of annihilation
how many ashes make a homeland?

NetaNyaope:

I bear the burden of security.
The right to defend
is that not sacred too?

These are surgical strikes,
smart bombs,
cleansing shadows from narrow alleys.

Their tunnels are threats.
Their breath is provocation.

Moloch *(mocking):*

Ah…
surgical like the blade on a baby's throat.
Smart — like fire raining on a hospital bed.
Your missiles hum lullabies of empire.

I drank blood from stone.
You distill it through hashtags.

You have mechanised me.
Made my hunger efficient.

NetaNyaope *(defensive, twitching):*

We warn them.
We leaflet the graves before we dig them.
They use their children as shields.
What choice do we have?

Moloch *(rising in flame):*

Choice?
You chose every bullet.
Every trembling gasp beneath rubble
is a vote cast for your decay.

Even I, demon of the ancients,
am startled by your justifications.
You do not sacrifice to gods.
You sacrifice to fear.

You've become addicted to it—
snorting power through the skulls of the innocent.

NetaNyaope *(stumbling)*:

I… I am democracy's gatekeeper.
A bulwark against savagery.
They burn too.

Moloch:

And yet they plant olive trees in broken concrete.
They carry their dead on shoulders, not drones.
They name their pain.
You… rename it collateral.

Your soul is embalmed in concrete.
You've not built a nation
you've built a morgue
with surveillance cameras.

Final Chorus *(offstage – BuSuSu voice)*:

From Sharpeville to Shuja'iyya,
we hear your fires.
But we do not kneel to them.

We walk backward through your smoke,
bone in hand, Sunsum on tongue.
We remember.
We entangle.
We sculpt the names you tried to erase.

Crayons in the Synapse
– A Neural Lament for the Bombed Child

Pitika Ntuli, Neuro-Sangoma of Hope

Now I re-enter the brain with reverence
where crayons become synaptic sparks,
and bombs are corrupted misfires
of ancestral memory.

How can a child still laugh
while gripping a crayon
that fragile wand of colour
as missiles tear through neurons of memory,
bombing dreams
from the brainstem up?

This is not just war
it is a neural atrocity.

The child's laughter,
bright with dopaminergic light,
is interrupted mid-sentence
by the scream of metal
that shatters synaptic trust.

A child's brain
still sculpting its pathways,
still learning the dance
of oxytocin and hope
is rewired
by fear,
by fire,
by flash.

And yet
the crayon persists.

In the grip of that tiny hand
lies limbic resistance
to annihilation.

The child's cortex
still imagines suns,
trees, families, peace.
Still paints in beta waves of becoming,
despite the electrical storms of grief.

Old men
with shriveled empathy centres
and brains fossilised in propaganda—
launch missiles
from thrones of disassociation.

They do not hear
the mirror neurons weeping.
They do not feel
the hippocampus shiver
with each child's scream
etched into the archive of trauma.

But we
we are the neurons who remember.
We are the Sunsum circuits
that refuse to forget.

The crayons are not broken.
They are neuro-electric testimonies
proof that laughter
once flowed
through the veins of time.

Wound in my Soul

In Gaza, I saw a girl child carried in a plastic bag
on the shoulders of a wounded grandmother
who walked a street littered with corpses!
Memories of Buchenwald and Treblinka
flooded my mind, memories toyed with me!
                I turned to gospel hymns to soothe my wounded soul.

Rumi came to me that night,
"Hope is the word," he whispered.
"I would like to see you dance without music."
In a corner of my room, my ancestral spirits nodded:
                "Be in search of spirit!"

In the stillness of night, visions filled my sight.
As a dance of sorrow and hope intertwined
in the depths of my soul, I sought the divine.
Rumi's words echoed:
                "Beyond suffering, find the sacred art."

With each step I felt the ancient rhythm,
the dance of wisdom.
My ancestors, guardians of the past,
gently whispered: "Seek the spirit.
                In the midst of darkness, be not misled."

In the silence, I found my prayer.
The girl in Gaza, the grandmother's pain,
became a sacred refrain.
Through the chaos, the strife brought
by marauding Zionist mercenaries,
I sought the spirit that gives life:
        Rumi's presence, a guiding light, in the darkest hours.

In this sacred space, five Vulindlela brothers hang—
they only wanted to live free in their ancestral land
with flowers, flowing rivers and splendid mountains.
In the dance of the mystics, poetry their music,
I find my peace – a connection that brings release
from anguish as I watch genocide at the hands of those
              who know that pain, but have forgotten to be human!

For Carlo Monteiro

Without you, I wouldn't write like this!
You held my hand in your mind,
guided me on the path of discovery:
a new language for my poetry.
You are Me, and I am You, we agreed.
Your mind dances like elementary particles,
your spirit pure as lucid dreams.
Now look what you make me write!

To the rhythm of throbbing drums,
beneath a canopy of tropical skies,
I seek a home in art, science & spirituality.
Each beat a sermon, a plea for justice
in troubled lands – Palestine, Ukraine,
Somalia, Afghanistan . . . world without end.

Embraced by electromagnetic waves,
love's energy pulses, soars above pettiness
to embrace the sun and moon of solace and joy!
In the season of genocide's grim despair,
in Gaza's heart where hate tears and ravages
blinding the worlds' eye of love as Zionist curses
heard in tunnels where hope disappears
make us sing a sacred chant.

In quantum's realm, where possibilities bloom,
we sculpt narratives dispelling the gloom.
Art, science and spirituality intertwining
to bring redemption for humankind.

Gaza at Dawn

Down in the deep valley
where night and day meet
in the phantom limb
of dismembered dreams . . .

there you found me reading
poems floating
like elemental particles of love
written on rugged rocks,
prophesying a future
where enemies will embrace
in a green valley with murals
of resplendent colour,
flowers smiling arias
in full-throated ease.

Suddenly a great noise!
Lightning and thunder?
            No!
Zionist bombs out for a stroll
leaving death and destruction,
children's limbs tossed
to the heavens silencing History,
statues mowed down
erasing memories of heroic moments
that spoke of our struggles and triumphs:
emblems of Resistance.

I calm myself with poems:
Mahmoud Darwish singing
under a cedar tree in Lebanon –
songs of his native land usurped –

and for now, a hopeful dawn
as day breaks sprinkling coolness,
waters of hope for a better life.

When the ANC and EFF Clashed in a Rally

When the ANC and EFF clashed in a rally,
a 9 year old girl caught a bullet.
She lies in a coma in hospital,
a verse from the bible reminding us
that the kingdom of heaven belongs
to children though we fail to protect them.

The suffering of innocents is a stark reminder
of our responsibility to nurture and shield
the next generation from political strife.
Gaza, a theatre of children's slaughter
where the most vulnerable among us
are easy targets for the Zionist genocidal drive!

As we witness the struggles of the young,
we are compelled to question the very fabric
of our society, asking if we've failed in our duty
to create a world where children are safe and thrive.
Now let us pray that the girl's journey
to the pearly gates is postponed indefinitely!

Another Child in Gaza

My mother's womb of love encodes
memories of my birth, night entangles
my fragmented dreams in capsules of thought.
I am a quantum particle oscillating
on waves of hope in a world losing coherence.

Televised genocide superposes echoes
that negate my existence. I am a child
standing on the remaining wall of our house
demolished by Israeli bombs.
No one observes my cries
as I seek my parents in the ruins.

Am I now an orphan like Sharif and Leila?
The wind collapses my wavefunction,
carries me far into a valley of nightmares.
Riding their terrors with impunity,
dare I superpose hope for a rebirth
into a world of love and joy?

The flames that devoured my school,
yesterday erased our mosque and hospital
killing my uncle and cousin.
What dreams do my child's mind
still encode for the future?

Yet I know my end will be a quantum leap
to a rebirth of hope for I carry the words
of our poets in the deep recesses
of my fevered and tortured soul.
And my homeland will not die despite their missiles!

But before I collapse, I must go to thank
the people of South Africa for their support.
I can smile a little now that Netanyaupe
is sweating for his diminishing career!

Memories of Genocide

I am a Herero child.
I carry memories of my people
driven off their land
to give way to German settlers.
The land of the Nama went
the same way!

Fields of skeletons decked our countryside
after a death march into the desert;
fields meant for farming
became concentration camps.
I knew then Black Lives did not matter –
a dress rehearsal for Auschwitz,
and Buchenwald and Treblinka
where millions were killed mercilessly!

But later I learnt Semitic lives
did not matter too!
Now it's the turn of Palestine:
humanity has no conscience!
Today children of the exterminated
become exterminators!

The world watches whilst Israelis feast
on the sight of children and women
dying from shrapnel, missiles
bombing hospitals in Gaza.

Mzansi took Netanyaupe to the ICJ
and America fumes!
They seek regime change in our land!
Now the world has become
a nightmare dancing on the tender
bodies of the innocent!

Is humanity so mad for dying?

The Plea of Spirit

I have become a spirit, Ase/Ashe,
providing the power and vibration for
change
in a world peddling demi-gods of
materialism,
greed and corruption.

I generate frequencies of hope
in burning places like Gaza!
I move unseen across borders without a
passport!
I move unheard, but felt in my breath
are whispers of ancestral voices
calling on us to open our arms
and embrace the future with fortitude.

In the face of oppression,
I am resilience and strength,
a beacon of light in the darkest hour
offering the oppressed courage to rise.

In the traditions of Ifa, Vodun, and Ubuntu,
I am the essence that binds us,
the unity of community and kinship.
I dwell in the sacred groves,
in the rituals of renewal and rebirth,
in the libations poured for the ancestors.

In the heartbeat of the earth,
in the breath of the wind,
I am ever-present.
Where wanton violence and death
breathe fumes of despair,
I am a testament to the enduring power
of Spirit.

Embrace me and all that is and ever was.
For I am Ase/Ashe:
the breath of life,
the spirit of change,
the power to transcend.

Become me!

Must We Die Needlessly?

Listening to Beethoven with my cat –
who loves gospel and classic –
the sheer beauty of the moment
sends my mind whirling,
tossing endless questions to myself.

How can a world of such beauty be so ugly!
How can humans be so anti-human!
How can genocide unfold before our very eyes
on every TV station worldwide,
and still be met by deafening silence?

How can religion – vessel of love and tolerance –
become an instrument of death
and wanton destruction as in Gaza?
How can we sleep and dream of sweet moments
whilst others weep at the hands of our loved ones?
Fathers unleashing fiery weapons
whilst cuddling their children!

I wrestle with conceptual violence.
We knew the pain we fought, resisted fiercely,
yet now we smile with those who killed us yesterday.
Our gods and ancestors hold our hands.
And so tomorrow, Palestinian and Zionist will smile
together!

We may perish in our thousands, but we will not let
hope die.
I think of Jewish friends here and in Israel
who only want to live, and dream of love and peace!

For Saber

You light the darkness with your love for Palestine,
defiance and resistance enveloping us in your clear vision.

We had our Bantustans here in Mzansi,
Sabras and Shatillas in Nyanga, Langa and Gugulethu.
Yet we resisted and defied the beasts
who cursed our days and nights.
And today, together with yesterday's foes,
we build a citadel of hope:
Slovo, Ruth First and Albie Sachs, Steven Sack,
all Jews who never forgot
the hellish smoke of crematoria
yet fought side by side with us,
sacrificing for the cause.

We fought not against white people,
but against a white power system.
Robert Mangaliso Sobukwe, arch Africanist, told us:
"There is only one race – the Human Race!"
guided by our ancestors and Nkulunkulu/Allah –
our God, the Cosmic Mind that unites us
in universal consciousness.

Saber, like a sharp sabre you slice
the darkness with your light;
your love for Palestine and your
defiant resistance, envelop us
in your vision of freedom.

Through mist-filled eyes,
we see clouds of longing for peace
rising in cascading waves.
We are both wave and particle,
photons and electrons dancing
under the full moon's glow,
awaiting the rebirth of freedom in Gaza.

Iconoclasts

In a Newtonian world, binary opposites rule supreme;
in the quantum world, interconnectedness reigns.
In Gaza, truth and memory are massacred
as creative and spiritual works of Art
are destroyed and the world merely watches.

In the daily dirge sung to Gaza's plight,
statues crumble, monuments weep,
mosques tremble in the fractured night –
a symphony of chaos, a cosmic war.
We hear and feel particles of history entangled in pain,
echoes of memory shattered in contempt.

In the realm where shadows rule, we listen diligently
to the poetry of loss and gain.
In Gaza's bombed out verse the past unfolds,
infinite possibilities and untold stories
rise out of the haze where truths are bold,
resilience emerges to tell a sad tale.

But amidst the quantum flux, spirits soar
guided by ancestors, unseen but heard.
In sacred whispers they find love
resonating, enduring and pure.
Gaza's defiant spirit a masterpiece
of strength and rising defiance!

Palestine will rise from the ashes:
didn't we in our land rise to demolish Apartheid?
We must wake from our sleep.

Now!

Isoseismal Shadows
– Memory as Seismic Resistance
*From Eichmann to NetaNyaope:
A Neural Indictment*

In the hippocampus of history,
a scar pulses – not past but present.

In Gaza, the neurons remember
what Auschwitz tried to erase;
what apartheid tried to drug into amnesia.

Two figures loom – not in ghostly hindsight
but in seismic parallel:
Eichmann, bureaucrat of genocide,
NetaNyaope, hallucinator of annihilation.

They do not walk side by side.
They vibrate on the same isoseismal fault line,
bound by dreams of *"final solutions."*

Eichmann said:
*"We do not hate them.
We only remove them."*

NetaNyaope mutters:
*"There are no civilians in Gaza.
Flatten it."*

Language and bullets.
Memory and rubble.
Papers signed in Berlin.
Drones launched over Rafah.
Same tremor.
Same synaptic silence.

What is a memory
if it cannot scream?

What is neuroscience
if it cannot indict
the electrochemical delusions
of power?

What are dreams
when they become blueprints
for obliteration?

This is not analogy.
This is entanglement.

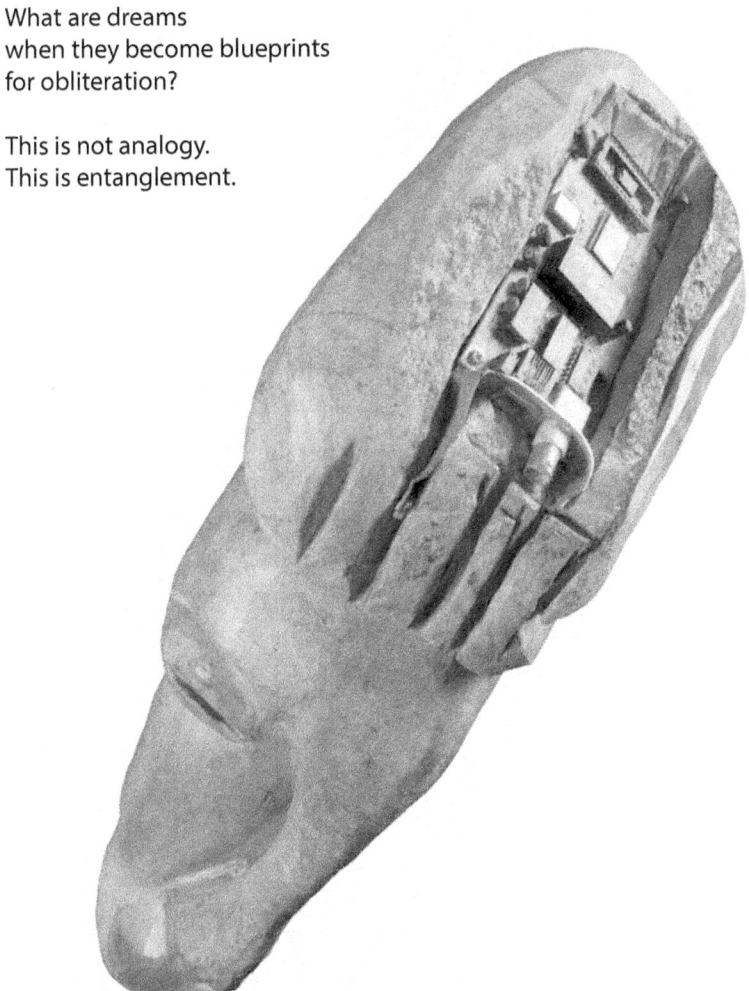

Of Faith Potential and Non-local Co-Relations

In the realm of power where shadows dwell,
Gaza's saga of anguish unfolds.
A plea for relief obscured by conflict's haze,
yet hope lingers in resilient ways.

From a far distance, non-local echoes
connect hearts in a universal dance.
In Gaza's turmoil, a cry for solace rises,
a longing for unity never ceases.

In the rubble and dust, dreams
take flight in the hearts of those
who hold onto the light that burns
night, dawn and day!

Potential, like a seed yearning to grow
in barren land, swells and spreads
non-local ties that bind us
across divides in the darkest night.

In Gaza's struggle, an epic of faith
and untold futures unfolds.
We must resolutely narrate and iterate!

Let faith guide the way through the storm.

NetanYaope vs The Prophet of BuSuSu
A Satirical Poetic Dialogue in Two Tongues and Infinite Truths

Scene: A Ruined Altar Between Two Worlds

Smoke rises.
A granite figure whispers.
Two voices.
One devours.
One remembers.

Voice 1: The Ghost of Moloch (NetanYaope)

I am fire in covenant's name.
My drones baptise the chosen soil.
I eat children for peace.

Their cries? Security alarms.
Their homes? Collateral syntax.

I sip from the cup of empire
its wine is white phosphorus.
And still, I am holy.

I do not kill, I "defend."

Gaza is my burnt offering.
Ask your silence
it worships me.

Voice 2: The Prophet of BuSuSu

Uqamba amanga, Moloch of Media Spin.
We see you
wrapped not in scrolls, but smokescreens.

We are the boneblowers of truth!
The sculptors of what you tried to erase.

That child you crushed beneath rubble?
Still speaks through my chisel.
That scream you silenced?

Now echoes in BuSuSu Province
where every junkyard nail is a witness.

Your dome may be iron,
but ours is spirit.

Thina Sobabili —
I and the bombed child,
the poet and the flame,
the last breath and the first drum.
—

Voice 1: NetanYaope (Sneering)

You throw metaphors like stones.
I return with tanks.
I have data. Diplomats.
And denial on demand.
—

Voice 2: Prophet of BuSuSu (Laughing)

And we have memory.
And the gods of dust.
And the Witness of Bone.

Your nyaope intoxicates parliaments—
but our clarity is ancestral.
You are Moloch with a blue tick.
I am BuSuSu with a bloodline.
The trickster is watching.
—

Final Chorus (Together)

We are not two.
We are the split mirror
One reveals terror,
the other truth shaped like a scar.

Thina Sobabili.
You devour.
We remember.

Pitika Ntuli is a renowned sculptor-poet whose work bridges the visceral weight of carved bone and stone with the lyrical fire of resistance poetry. His sculptures are vessels of ancestral memory and political testimony, forged in exile and honed in the crucible of African spirituality. His poetry moves between elegy and incantation — a voice that mourns, mocks, remembers, and reclaims. Blending satire, lament, and prophetic rage, Ntuli's verse is both invocation and weapon: shaped by Ubuntu, sharpened by Sumud, and carried on the breath of Sunsum. He is the Boneblower of the Living Stone — where art becomes ritual, and every poem is a return.

Botsotso Poetry since 2016

A Season of Tenderness and Dread – Abu Bakr Solomons
Loud and Yellow Laughter – Sindiswa Bususku-Mathese
The Colours of Our Flag – Allan Kolski Horwitz
The Alkalinity of Bottled Water – Makhosazana Xaba
On Days Such as This – Gail Dendy
Inhabiting Love – Abu Bakr Solomons
A History of Disappearance – Sarah Lubala
Hungry on Arrival – Kabelo Mofokeng
U Grand, Malume? – Sizakele Nkosi
Zabalaza Republic – Sihle Ntuli
Studies in Khoisan Verbs and other poems – Basil du Toit
Everybody is a Bridge – Anton Krueger
Igoli Egoli – Salimah Valiani
Down the Baakens Underworld – Brian Walter
A place to night in – Frank Meintjies
Flight of the Bird Spirit – Richard Cullinan
Maxwell the Gorilla and the Archbishop of Soshanguve – Angifi Proctor Dlaldla (on the Botsotso website)
Notes from the Dream Kingdom – KG Goddard
Rubble – Abu Bakr Solomons
Inside an Eyeball – Zeenit Saban-Jacobs
What is Owed? – Kelwyn Sole

www.ingramcontent.com/pod-product-compliance
Lightning Source LLC
Chambersburg PA
CBHW081005180426
43194CB00044B/2817